TEACH
love
INSPIRE
lead
MOTIVATE

CPSIA information can be obtained
at www.ICGtesting.com
Printed in the USA
BVHW010827200521
607787BV00011B/103

9 781979 586092